NATIONAL
GEOGRAPHIC
KiDS

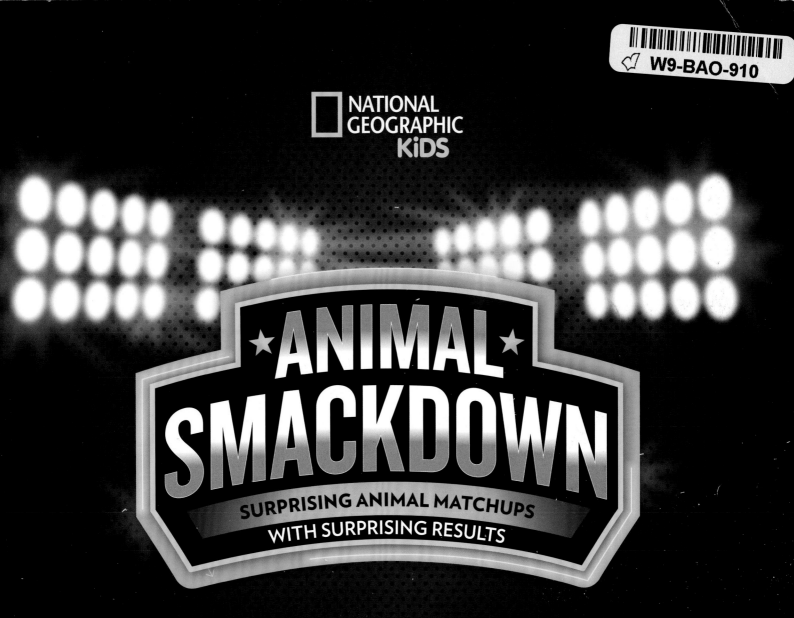

★ANIMAL★
SMACKDOWN

SURPRISING ANIMAL MATCHUPS
WITH SURPRISING RESULTS

EMILY KRIEGER

NATIONAL GEOGRAPHIC
WASHINGTON, D.C.

CONTENTS

PREHISTORIC
BADDIE

What if all of the winners in this book were to face off in a series of battles to **DETERMINE THE ULTIMATE ANIMAL?**

You'd have a bracket similar to those in sports tournaments, only with animals instead of athletes. Winners of each round advance to the next, until just one creature remains—the ultimate animal. Because there's an uneven number (15) of animals to start, one gets what's called a "bye" in sports: It gets to skip the first tournament and start playing in the second. In this case, that lucky player is the winner of the Fastest smackdown, whose speed would surely allow it to advance to the second round anyway. Who do you think will win the title of Ultimate Animal, and why? Make your guesses, then grab a parent and go online to *natgeokids.com/ animal-smackdown* to print and fill out a bracket, and then turn to the back of the book to see how it all shakes out!

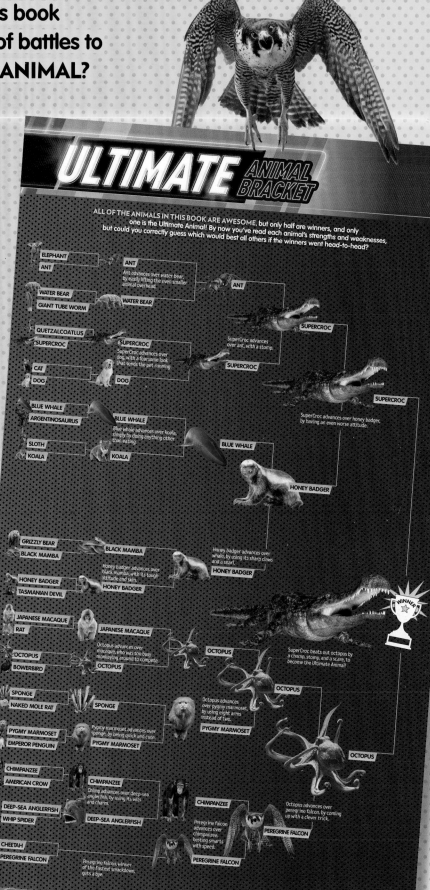

ULTIMATE ANIMAL BRACKET

ALL OF THE ANIMALS IN THIS BOOK ARE AWESOME, but only half are winners, and only one is the Ultimate Animal! By now you've read each animal's strengths and weaknesses, but could you correctly guess which would best all others if the winners went head-to-head?

ELEPHANT
ANT

ANT
Ant advances over water bear, by easily lifting the even smaller animal overhead.

ANT

WATER BEAR
GIANT TUBE WORM

WATER BEAR

SUPERCROC
SuperCroc advances over ant, with a stomp.

QUETZALCOATLUS
SUPERCROC

SUPERCROC
SuperCroc advances over dog, with a fearsome look that sends the pet running.

SUPERCROC

CAT
DOG

DOG

SUPERCROC
SuperCroc advances over honey badger, by having an even worse attitude.

BLUE WHALE
ARGENTINOSAURUS

BLUE WHALE
Blue whale advances over koala, simply by doing anything other than eating.

SLOTH
KOALA

KOALA

BLUE WHALE

HONEY BADGER

GRIZZLY BEAR
BLACK MAMBA

BLACK MAMBA

Honey badger advances over whale, by using its sharp claws and a snarl.

HONEY BADGER

HONEY BADGER
TASMANIAN DEVIL

HONEY BADGER
Honey badger advances over black mamba, with its tough attitude and skin.

JAPANESE MACAQUE
RAT

JAPANESE MACAQUE

OCTOPUS
BOWERBIRD

OCTOPUS
Octopus advances over macaque, who was too busy monkeying around to compete.

OCTOPUS

SUPERCROC beats out octopus by a chomp, stomp, and a scare, to become the Ultimate Animal!

SPONGE
NAKED MOLE RAT

SPONGE

OCTOPUS

Octopus advances over pygmy marmoset, by using eight arms instead of two.

PYGMY MARMOSET
EMPEROR PENGUIN

PYGMY MARMOSET
Pygmy marmoset advances over sponge, by being quick and cute.

PYGMY MARMOSET

OCTOPUS

CHIMPANZEE
AMERICAN CROW

CHIMPANZEE
Chimp advances over deep-sea anglerfish, by using its wits and charm.

CHIMPANZEE

Octopus advances over peregrine falcon, by coming up with a clever trick.

DEEP-SEA ANGLERFISH
WHIP SPIDER

DEEP-SEA ANGLERFISH

PEREGRINE FALCON
Peregrine falcon advances over chimpanzee, nestling smarts with speed.

PEREGRINE FALCON

CHEETAH
PEREGRINE FALCON

Peregrine falcon, winner of the Fastest smackdown, gets a bye.

PEREGRINE FALCON

WINNER

LAZIEST

INTRODUCTION

BEST PET

BEST PET

MOST TALENTED

HAVE YOU EVER IMAGINED TWO ANIMALS GOING TOE TO TOE TO DETERMINE WHO'S FASTEST, DEADLIEST, CLEVEREST, OR CUTEST? *National Geographic Kids Animal Smackdown* brings these matchups and more to life, pitting supersize and pint-size, present-day and prehistoric creatures against each other to see who would go home with the gold. Think predicting a winner would be easy? Think again: Seemingly dull animals can have hidden talents, small animals big abilities. In a battle for strength, could an ant best an elephant? Would a dog or a cat claim the title for best pet? Could a crow outsmart a chimp? Find out who would take first place in these face-offs in the following pages!

STRONGEST

DEADLIEST

TOUGHEST

STRONGEST

YOU MIGHT THINK THIS *BATTLE* HAS A *CLEAR* CHAMPION.

AFTER ALL, you have EARTH'S LARGEST LIVING LAND ANIMAL up against a SUPERSMALL INSECT. But hold off on picking a winner just yet. These mini but mighty insects might surprise you—sometimes a lightweight can beat a heavyweight!

ELEPHANT

❯ **FOR MILLENNIA,** people have used elephants to push, pull, pick up, and carry heavy things. With their strong trunks and legs, the big beasts have helped shaped history, aiding in everything from exploration to empire building. Ancient leaders even attacked enemies while riding atop elephants! There are two species of elephants—African and Asian—and while both are big, African elephants outweigh Asian ones by a few thousand pounds. These animals aren't all brawn, though. They're known for their brains, too, and are considered by scientists to be among the smartest and most social animals.

ELEPHANT VS ANT

ANT

> **A GREAT GENERAL** never rode into battle atop an ant. But the tiny insects are still tough, and in all sorts of weird ways. There are more than 12,000 species of ants worldwide. Some have jaws that snap shut faster than a shark's and others swarm and eat everything in their path. But ants are perhaps most famous for their ability to lift objects many times their own weight. Weaver ants made headlines for this in 2010, when a scientist snapped a photo of one holding a .018-ounce (.51-g) weight. To a human, that seems like nothing—it's the equivalent of hoisting a vitamin pill. But it's 100 times the ant's own weight … and on top of that, the athletic ant did it while upside down!

WHEN JUDGED ON PURE LIFTING ABILITY, IT SEEMS LIKE NO CONTEST: The African elephant is the winner, trunks down. But what about when you take body size into account? Take a look at these super stats and see who you think the champion is in the end.

ELEPHANTS EAT AS MUCH AS **300** POUNDS (136 KG) OF FOOD IN A SINGLE DAY.

ELEPHANT

TOUGH TRUNKS

An African elephant can carry more than 1,000 pounds (454 kg) on its back. But its trunk is tough, too: It can lift about 660 pounds (300 kg), or the weight of an adult grizzly bear! There are more than 150,000 muscles in a trunk but not a single bone, making the appendage powerful yet flexible. Fingerlike structures at the end of the trunk allow the super-strong animals to still gently pick up items as small as a peanut.

Elephants are able to lift so much weight because they themselves **WEIGH SO MUCH— LITERALLY TONS.** Even at birth, elephants are behemoths: about 200 pounds (91 kg) and three feet (0.9 m) tall! To help hold up all their weight, the animals have **EXTRA-THICK LEG BONES.**

HEFTY HEELS

An elephant's heels are a big help when it comes to lifting things. That's because they bear most of the brunt of the beasts' weight (and anything they're carrying). Big, fatty pads of tissue in the heels help distribute weight around the foot and absorb vibrations from the animals' big body movements.

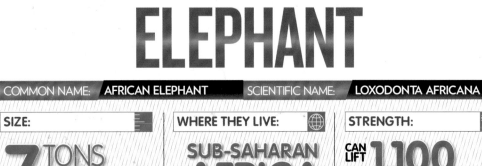

COMMON NAME: AFRICAN ELEPHANT	SCIENTIFIC NAME: LOXODONTA AFRICANA

SIZE:	WHERE THEY LIVE:	STRENGTH:
7 TONS (6,350 KG)	SUB-SAHARAN **AFRICA**	CAN LIFT **1,100** POUNDS (500 KG)

ANT

COMMON NAME: ASIAN WEAVER ANT   **SCIENTIFIC NAME:** OECOPHYLLA SMARAGDINA

SIZE:	WHERE THEY LIVE:	STRENGTH:
.0002 OUNCE (5 MG)	**ASIA AND AUSTRALIA**	CAN LIFT **.02** OUNCE (500 MG)

MIGHTY MOUTHS

Weaver ants use their heads when it comes to heavy lifting, but instead of a trunk, their mouths do the work. Superstrong muscles in the ants' heads power triangular, jaw-like mouthparts called mandibles that can lift humongous (to the ants, at least) loads.

GET A GRIP

When you're weightlifting, you don't want to be wobbly! On their feet, ants have tiny, moist pads that help them get a firm grip even on slippery surfaces. They can also lay down more of each foot, similar to how you spread your toes, to increase contact with the surface below.

Ants **WEIGH HARDLY ANYTHING** at all. They're tiny and lack bones. But when it comes to **WEIGHTLIFTING**, the insects' small size actually works to their advantage. Compared to elephants, **ANTS HAVE TO USE MUCH LESS MUSCLE POWER** to support their own weight. That leaves **MORE MUSCLE POWER** for lifting other objects.

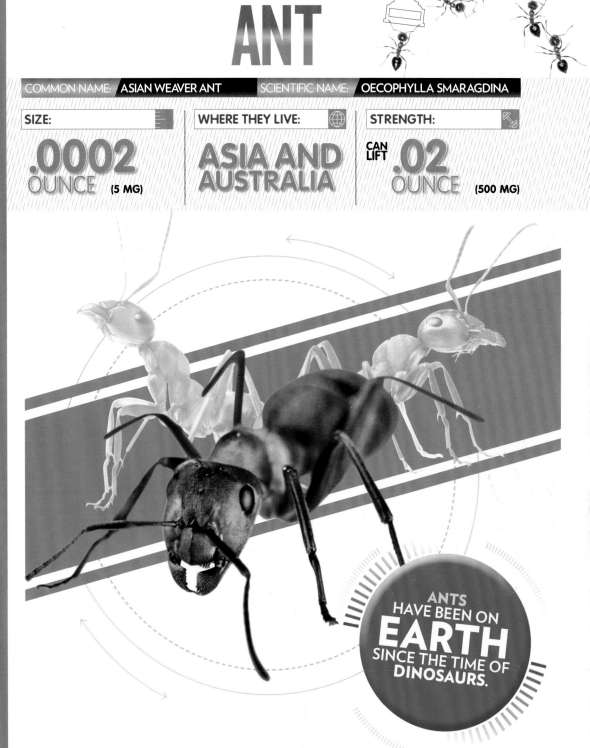

ANTS HAVE BEEN ON **EARTH** SINCE THE TIME OF **DINOSAURS.**

The elephant is one of the brawniest beasts in the animal kingdom. Elephants can lift about a million times more than ants. But the win goes to the animal that can hoist 100 times its own weight. For an elephant to do that, it would have to be able to pick up 1.3 million pounds (590 t), and it doesn't even come close! **IT'S A KNOCKOUT WIN FOR ANTS!**

EXTREME-LY STRONG ANIMALS

MORE SMALL BUT MIGHTY ANIMALS

These BEASTS may not look like much, but they have some SERIOUS BRAWN.

MANTIS SHRIMP

Who you callin' a shrimp? These crustaceans throw **STRONG, QUICK PUNCHES** that can reach speeds of up to 52 miles an hour (83 km/h) and **BREAK AQUARIUM GLASS!**

DUNG BEETLE

◀ Dung beetles are famous for **ROLLING POOP AROUND**—which is not only gross, it's apparently a lot of work. These beetles can pull 1,141 times their own weight!

HERO SHREW

▼ This aptly named little critter, which weighs at most only four ounces (115 g), **CAN WITHSTAND AN ADULT HUMAN STANDING ON ITS BACK,** thanks to a superstrong spine.

LIMPET

◀ These small snail relatives scrape algae off of seashore rocks with **TEENY-TINY TEETH** that are **STRONGER THAN KEVLAR,** the stuff in bulletproof vests!

CUTEST

THIS MAY BE THE MOST FUN MATCHUP EVER:

the world's SMALLEST MONKEY VS. the WORLD'S LARGEST PENGUIN in a furry vs. feathered battle to win the award for most adorable animal!

PYGMY MARMOSET

❯ **IMAGINE AN ADORABLE,** furry monkey tiny enough to fit in the palm of your hand. Meet the pygmy marmoset, the smallest monkey in the world. At only six inches (15 cm) tall, it packs a lot of personality into its bitty body.

Pygmy marmosets spend their days eating insects, lapping up tree sap, and chatting with and grooming each other high in the treetops of the Amazon rain forest. Listen closely and you may hear their high-pitched trills and squeaks. Look closely and you may see them making funny faces—it's a supercute way they communicate with each other!

PYGMY MARMOSET
VS
EMPEROR PENGUIN

EMPEROR PENGUIN

> **EMPEROR PENGUINS** are the largest penguins in the world, standing almost four feet (1.2 m) tall. Their endearing personalities and supercute chicks, like this one, have made them stars of the silver screen in movies like *March of the Penguins* and *Happy Feet*.

Emperor penguins form families in one of the harshest places on Earth: Antarctica during winter. But they have adorable ways of working together to keep warm when temperatures drop below zero. And they know how to have fun on the ice!

JUDGING BY LOOKS ALONE, BOTH PYGMY MARMOSETS AND EMPEROR PENGUINS ARE ADORABLE. But it's their personalities that will really make you say *Aww!*

PYGMY MARMOSETS HAVE SMALL HOME RANGES: THEY'LL SPEND THEIR **ENTIRE LIVES** IN JUST A FEW TREES.

LITTLE LOOKER
A big part of the pygmy marmoset's appeal is its small size. Everything about this mini monkey—which is only about as heavy as a stick of butter—is delightfully teeny. Their tails are the biggest things about them: At nine inches (23 cm), they're longer than the monkey's body!

CUTE COMMUNICATION
Pygmy marmosets make high-pitched trills and squeaks to talk to each other. Some of these sounds are so high humans are unable to hear them. The monkeys also make faces—moving their lips, eyelids, and ears—to show they're surprised, afraid, or content.

When two pygmy marmosets pair up, **THEY DO SO FOR LIFE.** Young marmosets tend to stick with their families until they're ready to start one of their own. **DADS HELP DELIVER BABIES** and then carry them around piggyback for the first two weeks of their life. Like other primates, pygmy marmosets spend a lot of time grooming each other's fur—**THEY LIKE TO LOOK GOOD!**

WINNER

PYGMY MARMOSET

COMMON NAME:	PYGMY MARMOSET	SCIENTIFIC NAME:	CALLITHRIX PYGMAEA

SIZE:

WHERE THEY LIVE:

6 INCHES TALL (15 CM)

AMAZON
RAIN FOREST

HUDDLE UP

In Antarctica, wind chill can drop temperatures to minus 76°F (-60°C)! To stay warm, emperor penguins huddle together. Individuals politely rotate being on the outside of the penguin pack, where it's windier and colder. Inside the pack, it's toastier and all those bodies block the wind.

Baby emperor penguins **WEIGH LESS THAN A POUND (0.4 KG)** at birth and aren't very fluffy at first—so they spend most of their time atop their dad's feet. But within a few months they grow a thick down that turns them into **FAT LITTLE FUZZBALLS** and contenders for the most adorable animal babies ever!

SMOOTH MOVES

Penguins can't fly. But they've still got moves. These tubby, kid-size birds waddle, a rocking, side-to-side walk that to most people is super cute. When they get tired of waddling, they slide—on their bellies! Living on ice poses a lot of challenges, but being able to slide down or across a long stretch of land is a big plus.

EMPEROR PENGUIN

COMMON NAME: EMPEROR PENGUIN   SCIENTIFIC NAME: APTENODYTES FORSTERI

SIZE:

4 FEET TALL (1.2 M)

WHERE THEY LIVE:

ANTARCTICA

EMPEROR PENGUINS CAN DIVE 1,850 FEET (565 M) **BELOW** THE **SEA** SURFACE—FARTHER THAN ANY OTHER BIRD.

Penguins, especially baby ones, are really popular animals. But pygmy marmosets are adorably small furballs their entire lives. Plus their personalities are awesome, too. Just look at those funny faces! **WE'RE CROWNING THESE MICRO MONKEYS THE WINNER!**

MORE CUTE PETITE PRIMATES (YOU MAY NOT KNOW ABOUT!)

Tiny faces, tiny hands — these POCKET-SIZE PRIMATES are TOO CUTE!

GOLDEN LION TAMARIN

 With their **FLOWING MANES**, these teeny-tiny primates look like **MINI LIONS**. Dads love to carry their babies around on their backs.

COQUEREL'S SIFAKA

These lemurs are only about 18 inches (45 cm) tall but use their powerful hind legs to **JUMP MORE THAN 30 FEET** (9 m)!

PYGMY MOUSE LEMUR

The world's smallest primate could **FIT INSIDE A TEACUP** and stands at most five inches (13 cm) tall.

PHILIPPINE TARSIER
Each of these primate's **SUPERSIZE EYES** is about as big as a marble!

ANGOLAN DWARF GALAGO
> This six-inch (15-cm)-tall species wasn't discovered by scientists until 2017, after they heard its **UNFAMILIAR CALLS** in a forest in Angola.

COMMON MARMOSET
> These polite primates **WAIT THEIR TURN TO TALK,** a behavior marmoset babies learn from their parents, scientists recently discovered.

SMARTEST

IN A BATTLE OF WITS, WHO WOULD WIN — A CHIMP OR A CROW?

CHIMPS are some of our closest relatives—and not to brag, but we humans are known for our brainpower! But CROWS are seriously smart, too. Scientists studying both animals have uncovered some impressive ways in which they use their noggins. BUT WHO WILL WIN THIS MENTAL MATCHUP?

CHIMPANZEE

❯ CHIMPANZEES and humans share about 99 percent of the same DNA, or genetic information. That's why scientists say chimps are our "cousins." These cousins swing and knuckle-walk (and sometimes even walk upright!) in forests, woodlands, and grasslands across sub-Saharan Africa.

In their research, scientists have uncovered a lot about chimps that looks familiar: They too solve problems, make and use tools, hunt in groups, and can even learn sign language and play computer games!

AMERICAN CROW

> **PEOPLE OFTEN UNDERESTIMATE CROWS** because they're birds. But stop and watch them for a while, and you'll see what scientists have for decades: Animals able to solve problems, make and use tools, and recognize people's faces, among other feats.

Crow species, of which there are many, live on every continent except South America and Antarctica. Scientists who study and talk about crow smarts are often referring to two types of crow: American crows (found in North America) and New Caledonian crows (found on a few South Pacific islands).

CHIMPANZEE **VS** ★ ★ AMERICAN CROW

SCIENTISTS THINK CHIMPS AND CROWS ARE SOME OF EARTH'S BRAINIEST BEASTS. BUT HOW EXACTLY DO THEY USE THEIR HEADS? When it's time to pick a winner, think carefully—your answer could reveal how smart you are!

CHIMPS CAN RECOGNIZE EACH OTHER FROM **BEHIND,** BY MEMORIZING WHAT EACH OTHER'S BEHINDS LOOK LIKE!

SIGNS OF INTELLIGENCE

Chimps use body language, vocalizations, and facial expressions to communicate with each other. When it comes to talking to humans, a few chimps have learned a neat trick: American Sign Language. One chimp, named Washoe, learned about 250 signs!

AMAZINGLY, chimps have bested people in perhaps the most people-like of pursuits: **COMPUTER GAMES!** Chimps' excellent memories, ability to recognize patterns, and competitive skills likely all contribute to their being **BETTER THAN HUMAN ADULTS** at playing basic computer games in scientific studies on ape smarts.

CHIMPANZEE

TOOLIN' AROUND

Chimps make and use a variety of tools to fetch themselves something to eat. They'll use stones to crack open nuts. They'll strip the leaves off a twig and use it as a fishing pole to get termites out of a hole. And they'll sharpen branches into "spears" that they use to hunt for small animals.

COMMON NAME:	CHIMPANZEE	SCIENTIFIC NAME:	PAN TROGLODYTES

SIZE:

70-130 POUNDS (31-59 KG)

WHERE THEY LIVE:

SUB-SAHARAN **AFRICA**

In separate studies, **WILD CROWS** and **CHILDREN** were presented with a problem: **HOW TO USE GIVEN OBJECTS,** such as rocks, to raise the water levels in clear containers. Kids struggled to solve the problem, but **A CROW NAMED KITTY CRACKED IT!**

NO HANDS, NO PROBLEM

Even though they don't have hands, crows are surprisingly good at making and using tools. Some have been spotted using pieces of leaves to stick into tree crevices to retrieve tasty morsels. The crows tear these leaf tools into specific shapes perfect for the task. They've also been known to use their beaks to bend twigs into hooks for fishing out food.

Researchers in Seattle, Washington, U.S.A., **WORE MASKS** while catching and releasing crows on a college campus. Those crows not only **REMEMBERED WHICH FACE WAS A FOE—** they also spread the word! When the masked scientists returned to campus, **CROWS SWOOPED AND CAWED ALARMS**—even ones that hadn't been caught!

AMERICAN CROW

COMMON NAME: **AMERICAN CROW** SCIENTIFIC NAME: **CORVUS BRACHYRHYNCHOS**

SIZE:

0.8-1
POUND (363-455 G)

WHERE THEY LIVE:

NORTH AMERICA

SOME SCIENTISTS THINK CROWS ARE AS **SMART** AS APES.

Crows are brainiacs, no doubt about it. But when it comes to intelligence, **CHIMPS WIN:** They can learn sign language and beat adult humans at computer games! Stay tuned, though: Some scientists say crows and chimps are neck and neck when it comes to smarts and are crafting new puzzles to probe the animals' intelligence.

DEMON FISH: **DEEP-SEA ANGLERFISH** OVERSIZE CREEPY-CRAWLY: **WHIP SPIDER**

ARE YOU *AFRAID* OF ANIMALS THAT LOOK LIKE *DEMONS* AND OVERSIZE *SPIDERS* THAT DWELL IN THE DARK?

Then you should skip ahead a few pages. Because you're about to learn about two of the creepiest animals ever: **WHIP SPIDERS** and **DEEP-SEA ANGLERFISH!**

DEEP-SEA ANGLERFISH

> **DEEP-SEA ANGLERFISH** swim more than a mile (1.6 km) below the sea surface, where the sun's rays don't reach. They find prey in the pitch-black with the help of a long dorsal spine that arcs over their heads and dangles in front of their mouths. At its tip a lure lit up by glowing bacteria attracts curious fish, which quickly end up a meal.

But the creep factor doesn't stop there. These fish have gaping maws filled with razor-sharp teeth, and they look like semitransparent goblins. They're so creepy they seem unreal. But you'd better believe it— there are more than 150 species found in every ocean on Earth.

WHIP SPIDER

> **WHIP SPIDERS** look like they're part spider, part insect, and part alien. They're none of those things, though. Instead, they're something called an amblypygid, which, like spiders, are part of the class of creatures called arachnids. Think of them as a creepy-crawly the size of an adult human hand, with eight eyes, claws, and fanglike mouthparts. They're carnivores and detect their prey in the dark with the help of long antennae.

There are some 150 species of whip spiders. They are nocturnal and live everywhere from deserts to rain forests. In spite of their formidable appearance, they are actually quite shy. Thank goodness!

DEEP-SEA ANGLERFISH
VS
WHIP SPIDER

THINK YOU'RE SPOOKED NOW? Just wait—these creatures get even creepier.

AN ANGLERFISH'S **TEETH** ANGLE INWARD TO PREVENT PREY FROM **ESCAPING.**

BIG MOUTH

Anglerfish look like swimming goblins, with their oversize heads, jutting jaws, and sharp teeth that sometimes look tangled. The fish's mouths are big for a reason: the better to gobble prey up to twice their own size!

ANGLERFISH SWEETHEARTS stay together for life. But it's not as sweet as it sounds. Through growths on its snout and jaw, the male **ATTACHES HIMSELF** to a female's body **AND NEVER LETS GO.** Stuck to her side, most of his major organs **MELT AWAY** and his blood mingles with hers, until he becomes a **LIVING, BREATHING LITERAL CLINGY BOYFRIEND** for the rest of his life.

WINNER

DEEP-SEA ANGLERFISH

COMMON NAME:	DEEP-SEA ANGLERFISH	SCIENTIFIC NAME:	CERATIOIDEI ORDER

SIZE:

TYPICALLY LESS THAN

3 FEET

(0.9 M)

WHERE THEY LIVE:

BELOW ABOUT 1,000 FEET (300 M) IN

EVERY OCEAN

ON EARTH

COME CLOSER

What's creepier than a scary-looking fish with big, sharp teeth that swims around in the dark? A fanged fish that can trick other animals into swimming right up to its mouth! Anglerfish do this with a built-in fishing pole: a spine on their back that arcs over their heads. A glowing orb of bacteria attracts passing critters. When they get close: chomp!

WHIP SPIDER

LACKING IN LOOKS
Poor whip spiders—they've got a lot of features that freak people out. They look like XXL spiders encased in armor and have spiky, sometimes huge, claws. As if that weren't enough, they also have eight eyes and whip-like antennae that waggle in front of them and reach as much as 10 inches (25 cm) in length.

SEEING GHOSTS
Whip spiders molt, or shed, their exo-skeleton as they grow and it becomes too tight. What they leave behind—a whitish, semi see-through perfect shell of their former selves—has the unsettling appearance of something even scarier than a whip spider: a whip spider ghost!

WHIP SPIDERS walk sideways. For a lot of people, there's something about an animal skittering from side to side that's **JUST PLAIN CREEPY.** Perhaps it's because they move in a direction you hadn't anticipated, which gives the impression the critter could **CRAWL UP ON YOU** when you least expect it.

| COMMON NAME: | WHIP SPIDER | SCIENTIFIC NAME: | AMBLYPYGI ORDER |

SIZE:

BODY: 1.2 TO 2 INCHES (3-5 CM). LEGS CAN BE
10 INCHES
(25 CM)

WHERE THEY LIVE:

EVERY
CONTINENT
EXCEPT ANTARCTICA

WHIP SPIDERS HAVE BEEN AROUND FOR MORE THAN **300** MILLION YEARS.

They both look scary and dwell in darkness. But anglerfish are bigger, so a bite from one would probably hurt worse than a pinch from a whip spider. And there may be nothing creepier than two animals fusing together for life and sharing blood. **SO THE FREAKY FISH WINS!**

MORE SPOOKY ANIMALS

Not all animals are cute and cuddly. You wouldn't want
to run into these CREEPY CRITTERS in the dark!

GOBLIN SHARK

More than 4,000 feet (1,200 m) down in the pitch-
dark ocean swims this 12-foot (3.6-m) shark with a
MOUTH FULL OF SPINY SCRAGGLY TEETH.

MARABOU STORK

This bird can get to be as big as a 12-year-old kid! It **DINES ON DEAD ANIMALS,** garbage, and large, living animals such as adult flamingos.

GOLIATH BIRD-EATING TARANTULA

This spider's name says it all: **IT'S HUGE** (up to a foot [0.3 m] long!), it eats birds, and it's hairy.

GIANT AMAZON LEECH

THE WORLD'S LARGEST LEECH reaches a foot and a half (.45 m) in length and uses a six-inch (15-cm)-long proboscis to suck blood from other animals.

LARGE FLYING FOX

You might think **VAMPIRES** are real if you saw a group of these bats with five-foot (1.5-m) wingspans hanging upside down from a tree.

GIANT WETA

The world's **LARGEST INSECT** weighs about as much as three mice and can eat a full-size carrot.

GROUCHIEST

| SOLO SCRAPPER: | HONEY BADGER | MANIAC MARSUPIAL: | TASMANIAN DEVIL |

HONEY BADGER

HONEY BADGERS' name may sound sweet, but these mammals are anything but. Their name refers to their taste not for honey but for bee babies, called larvae, found with the sweet stuff. But badgers eat anything and everything, even venomous snakes and cheetah cubs! Honey badgers spend most of their time solo, roaming deserts, forests, and grasslands in Africa and Asia in search of food. Snooping around everything from beehives to lion dens leads to a lot of trouble. A honey badger often wins a fight, though, even against larger animals, thanks to its superstrong teeth, jaws, claws, and skin, and a lot of bluster.

SOME ANIMALS ARE REAL *GROUCHES*, ALWAYS GETTING INTO FIGHTS AND ON OTHER ANIMALS' NERVES.

Among the most famously foul-tempered are
HONEY BADGERS and TASMANIAN DEVILS.
Both of these cranks have bad attitudes, but which is worse?

HONEY BADGER VS TASMANIAN DEVIL

TASMANIAN DEVIL

> **THEIR NAME SAYS IT ALL:** Tasmanian devils have a devilish personality. Though they resemble little bears, these nocturnal marsupials aren't very cuddly. They howl, snarl, snap their jaws, let loose foul odors, bite, fight, and fly into rages that have them literally spinning in circles. Like honey badgers, Tasmanian devils are largely solitary creatures. These carnivores come together to feed on found carcasses, but otherwise they spend most of their time prowling the wilds of Tasmania on their own. Also like honey badgers, devils have powerful jaws and teeth, which they use to eat every part of an animal, including fur, bones, and organs.

HONEY BADGERS AND TASMANIAN DEVILS HAVE A LOT IN COMMON: They're about the same size, they're feisty, and they have irritating behaviors—and, not surprisingly, they're both loners. If they weren't such grumps, perhaps they could even be pals! But which would be worse to befriend?

HONEY BADGER SKIN IS SO LOOSE THAT IF AN ENEMY GRABS ON, THEY CAN **SQUIRM** AROUND AND BITE BACK!

FREQUENT FIGHTS

Honey badgers are always poking their noses in places they don't belong, looking for food or a place to rest. All that poking around often leads to dustups with other, unpleasantly surprised animals. But honey badgers don't back down. They sometimes take on much bigger animals like lions and leopards—and win!

STEALING HOME

How would you feel if you came home and another kid had taken over your room? That's exactly what a honey badger does to aardvarks, mongooses, foxes, and other animals when it decides to call dibs on their homes. The badgers can dig their own dens, too. But why build when you can steal a home that's move-in ready?

HONEY BADGER

WINNER

HONEY BADGERS STINK. No, really: **A SCENT GLAND** in the animal's bum releases an odor similar to that of a **SKUNK'S.** The badgers release the **FUNK** when they **FEEL THREATENED** or to mark their territory. Their poop reeks of it, too.

COMMON NAME:	HONEY BADGER	SCIENTIFIC NAME:	MELLIVORA CAPENSIS

SIZE:

10-30 POUNDS (4-13 KG)

WHERE THEY LIVE:

AFRICA AND **ASIA**

TASMANIAN DEVIL

COMMON NAME: **TASMANIAN DEVIL**	SCIENTIFIC NAME: **SARCOPHILIS HARRISII**

SIZE:

10-30 POUNDS (4-13 KG)

WHERE THEY LIVE:

AUSTRALIAN ISLAND OF
TASMANIA

Getting some shut-eye on the island of TASMANIA might be hard, thanks to the LOUD, EERIE SHRIEKS Tasmanian devils make at night. The sounds alone are AWFUL. But hearing them in the middle of the night is DOUBLY SCARY—because the DEVILS HOWL when SHARING A CARCASS!

FEISTY AND FRIENDLESS

Tasmanian devils are rightly famous for the rages they can fly into. Although they are typically loners, a threatened devil will snarl, lunge, whirl in circles, open its mouth (the better to see its big, sharp teeth), and when all else fails, deliver one of the strongest bites of any mammal.

STINK BOMB

Tasmanian devils, like honey badgers, have a secret, stinky weapon. When stressed, devils release a funky, foul odor from a gland on their bum. If their bad tempers don't ward off other animals, the stench might do the trick.

A TASMANIAN DEVIL CAN EAT UP TO **40 PERCENT OF ITS WEIGHT** IN ONE DAY!

Deciding which of these two animals has the worst temperament is a tough call. Both could be pretty unpleasant to run into in the wild. But honey badgers are the only ones that hijack homes! **SO, THE BADGERS TAKE THE TITLE OF GROUCHIEST ANIMAL—WHAT AN HONOR!**

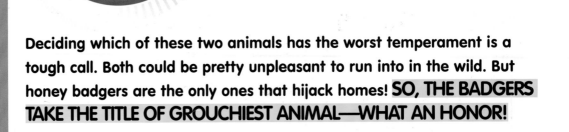

YOU'RE ABOUT TO MEET TWO ANIMALS THAT ARE TOUGHER

than any shark, grizzly, or crocodile. WATER BEARS and DEEP-SEA TUBE WORMS take tough to the next level: They're able to stay alive in crazy conditions that kill most animals!

WATER BEAR

> **WATER BEARS** aren't really bears. They're the world's smallest visible animal, an eight-legged invertebrate not even the size of a poppy seed that resembles a teeny-tiny teddy bear ... if that teddy bear were as indestructible as The Terminator. To find one, collect a clump of moss or lichen and look closely. Believe it or not, possibly ambling about on there is one of the world's toughest animals! Scientists are busy studying how water bears bounce back from being frozen, boiled, dried out, starved, and even shot into space.

GIANT TUBE WORM

> **TO FIND A DEEP-SEA TUBE WORM,** you'll have to travel more than a mile below the sea surface, to a pitch-dark, chilly seafloor blasting superhot plumes of toxic chemicals from deep within Earth. In the midst of this hostile habitat live six-foot (1.8-m)-long worms, each hidden within a white tube attached to the seafloor. These worms don't look tough. But in fact, they live in conditions so extreme that scientists study them to try to figure out what life on other planets might be like.

WATER BEAR
VS
GIANT TUBE WORM

A HUMAN CAN'T SURVIVE BEING FROZEN, BOILED, OR STARVED—but those conditions barely make these contenders blink. So which is the winner?

REPORTEDLY, A SAMPLE OF **100-YEAR-OLD** DEHYDRATED TARDIGRADES WAS BROUGHT BACK TO LIFE.

WATER BEAR

WINNER

COMMON NAME: **WATER BEAR, OR TARDIGRADE** SCIENTIFIC NAME: **PHYLUM TARDIGRADA**

SIZE:

WHERE THEY LIVE:

MARINE, FRESHWATER, AND DAMP ENVIRONMENTS

.004-.02

INCH (0.1-0.5 MM)

EVERYWHERE

ON EARTH

BITTY BEARS IN SPACE
Water bears have an awesome achievement: They're the first animals to survive the vacuum (that means no air), radiation blasts, and freezing temperatures of space. Scientists shot the tiny critters into space in 2007, aboard a satellite. There they floated in special containers 167 miles (270 km) above sea level for 10 days before plummeting back to Earth. Upon inspection, most were A-OK. And a few were even able to survive radiation blasts 700 times stronger than the sun's rays on Earth!

EXTREME LIVING
When you're a water bear, there's not much you can't take. The teeny-tiny creatures can survive extreme temperatures, ranging from minus 328°F (-200°C) to 304°F (151°C). And despite preferring wet places, they can tough it out during a drought. Imagine a fish that can live on land for years!

To survive harsh conditions, **WATER BEARS** do something **REALLY WEIRD:** They transform themselves into **GLASSLIKE, BALL-SHAPED, BARELY ALIVE CRITTERS.** They can stay in this state for a **DECADE OR MORE** before going back to a normal life.

IN HOT WATER

Deep-sea tube worms live near openings in the seafloor that spew plumes of superheated water—up to 750°F (400°C)!—laced with chemicals like hydrogen sulfide and ammonia. There aren't many animals that could survive these hot, toxic blasts. But amazingly, the worms not only don't mind them, they actually depend on them to stay alive!

NO FOOD, NO PROBLEM

Tube worms don't eat—ever! That may sound impossible, but these worms have developed a neat trick: They get all the nutrients they need from bacteria living inside them. Because the worms don't eat, they have no mouth, no digestive tract, and no bum. Also absent: eyes. These worms keep things simple. Maybe that's the secret to being tough!

A deep-down seafloor existence is tough: It comes with **CRUSHING PRESSURE**, about 250 times what you experience on land. Plus, there's **NO SUNLIGHT**, and **WATER TEMPERATURES** are **ALMOST FREEZING!**

GIANT TUBE WORM

COMMON NAME: **DEEP-SEA, OR GIANT, TUBE WORM**   SCIENTIFIC NAME: **RIFTIA PACHYPTILA**

SIZE:

UP TO
6 FEET TALL (1.8 M)

WHERE THEY LIVE:

EASTERN
PACIFIC OCEAN
SEAFLOOR

DEEP-SEA TUBE WORMS, DESPITE NOT EATING, CAN **GROW** AT A RATE OF MORE THAN TWO FEET (0.6 M) A YEAR!

Both water bears and deep-sea tube worms have an arsenal of alien-like abilities that redefine what it means to be an animal. **BUT THERE CAN BE ONLY ONE WINNER. AND WATER BEARS ARE IT—THEY CAN SURVIVE BEING SHOT INTO SPACE! THEIR TOUGHNESS IS LITERALLY OUT OF THIS WORLD!**

EXTREME-LY TOUGH ANIMALS

THESE ANIMALS MAY NOT LOOK LIKE MUCH, BUT THEY HAVE SUPERPOWERS

that allow them to live through EXTREME COLD, HEAT, and other conditions that would kill most animals!

BDELLOID ROTIFER
✔ If these microscopic, aquatic animals feel threatened, **THEY COMPLETELY DRY THEMSELVES OUT** and catch a ride on the wind to a safer spot!

BRINE SHRIMP
◀ Freshwater shrimp that live in Utah's Great Salt Lake, U.S.A., swim in water that's **10 TIMES SALTIER** than the ocean!

GLACIAL ICE WORM
These wrigglers **SPEND THEIR ENTIRE LIVES ON GLACIER ICE—BRRRR!** They die if the temperature climbs to just 40°F (4°C)!

HIMALAYAN JUMPING SPIDER
◀ When you live higher up than any other animal—**MORE THAN FOUR MILES (6.4 KM) ABOVE SEA LEVEL**—the only food you can find is whatever insects a breeze blows up the mountain!

SAHARA DESERT ANT
⌃ These little insects skitter across sands that reach **140°F** (60°C) without burning their feet!

WOOD FROG
⌃ These frogs literally chill during winter: **THEIR BODIES FREEZE UPON FIRST FROST** and thaw months later when the weather's nicer!

COCKROACH
Incredibly, these creepy-crawlies can **LIVE WITHOUT A HEAD FOR WEEKS!**

MANGROVE KILLIFISH
⌃ When their watery homes dry out, these fish flip themselves head-over-tail across land to a pile of damp leaves or logs, **WHERE THEY LIVE FOR MONTHS BREATHING AIR THROUGH THEIR SKIN!**

MOST TALENTED

EIGHT-ARMED TALENT: **OCTOPUS** | TRIPLE-THREAT BIRD: **BOWERBIRD**

THINK YOUR PET KNOWS TRICKS?

Try putting it up against an **OCTOPUS** or a **BOWERBIRD** in an animal talent show. Their tricks include mimicking the sound of people talking, squeezing into impossibly small spaces, and disappearing before your very eyes!

OCTOPUS

> **YOU MAY BE WONDERING** what kind of an act an octopus would put on at a talent show. Juggling? Abstract ink painting? Disappearing? All of these are good guesses. But these sea creatures have a lot of other tricks, too.

Hundreds of species of octopuses live in all of the oceans on Earth. They're especially abundant in warm waters. Most live near the seafloor, where they hunt for prey with the help of their eight long, suckered arms. When threatened, octopuses can squirt black ink or quickly camouflage themselves for a speedy getaway.

BOWERBIRD

> **IF AN ANIMAL COULD BE A POP STAR,** a bowerbird would be it. These talented birds sing, dance, and bling out their custom-built homes. They "tweet," too, of course!

Twenty species of bowerbirds are found on the island of New Guinea and in Australia. They're named after the impressive structures, called bowers, males build to woo females. Males go to great lengths to build the best bower possible, sometimes constructing towers up to nine feet (2.7 m) tall! But they don't stop there. They then comb the forests they live in for treasures—everything from flowers to dead insects to toys—to decorate their bowers!

OCTOPUS
VS
★ ★
BOWERBIRD

OCTOPUSES ARE AMONG THE SMARTEST INVERTEBRATES ON EARTH, and they've got the skills to prove it. But bowerbirds bring a lot of talent to the table, too.

SOME OCTOPUSES **CAN RUN ON LAND.**

OCTOPUS

WINNER

COMMON NAME:	OCTOPUS	SCIENTIFIC NAME:	OCTOPODA ORDER

SIZE:

WHERE THEY LIVE:

LESS THAN
1 OUNCE (1G) **-600** POUNDS (272 KG)

ALL OF THE WORLD'S
OCEANS

ESCAPE ARTISTS
Octopuses are squishy. This comes in handy when trying to squeeze a 600-pound (272-kg) body through a hole the size of a quarter, which these sea creatures can do. Because of this, they're sneaky escape artists that have busted loose from aquariums all over the world.

MASTERS OF DISGUISE
Octopuses are master mimics. If one feels threatened or wants to sneak up on prey, it can change its skin to completely blend in with the environment—everything from coral to kelp to sandy seafloors—in less than a second. It's possible to never see an octopus coming or going, even though it's right in front of your eyes!

If you need a hand with something, **ASK AN OCTOPUS.** Their arms are surprisingly **STRONG AND NIMBLE** (plus, there are eight of them). They **LIKE TO TINKER,** and they're **FAST LEARNERS.** They can quickly figure out how to unscrew jar lids, open latches, and even **OPEN A SERIES OF LOCKS!**

BOWERBIRD

BOWERBIRDS not only build their **COMPLICATED BOWERS**, they also **DECORATE THEM.** Bowers can be tall, twiggy towers, alleys, or tunnels built from plant material, or cleared spaces that look like a courtyard. All are decorated with found objects, often with an emphasis on **SHINY STUFF**, such as tinfoil, mirrors, and CDs, sure to win the hearts of female bowerbirds.

| COMMON NAME: | BOWERBIRD | SCIENTIFIC NAME: | PTILONORHYNCHIDAE FAMILY |

SIZE:

ALL WEIGH LESS THAN A
POUND (.45 KG),
ARE 9-15 INCHES (24-37 CM) LONG

WHERE THEY LIVE:

NEW GUINEA AND
AUSTRALIA

VERY IMPRESSIVE VOCALS

If you're in the forests of New Guinea and hear the sounds of a pig, waterfall, or people chatting, think twice—it may be bowerbirds making all of those noises! They're expert mimics, able to realistically replicate human-made, environmental, and other animal sounds.

MALE BOWERBIRDS **TEAR DOWN** EACH OTHER'S BOWERS AND STEAL EACH OTHER'S DECORATIONS.

DANCING MACHINES

Bowerbirds don't just dance. Their fancy footwork is so complex that it could be considered choreography. They dance to attract a mate, so having impressive moves is important. These include sways, bobs, hops, and weird wing waves, all performed at their bowers.

Both animals have got talent. The tough call is deciding who's got more. **IN THE END, OCTOPUSES WIN,** with their abilities to practically disappear, slip in to and out of crazy-small spaces, and tinker with and take things apart!

MORE AMAZING OCTOPUS FACTS

An amazing fact for each of the ANIMAL'S ARMS!

1
OCTOPUSES ARE COLORBLIND— and yet still able to change colors to blend in with their surroundings.

2
Octopus ink doesn't just create a black cloud that conceals; it also contains a CHEMICAL that SCRAMBLES SEA CREATURES' SENSES.

3

Octopus ink sometimes **FORMS A SHAPE** that resembles the **EIGHT-ARMED SEA CREATURE.** This faux octopus fools predators.

4

ALL OCTOPUSES ARE VENOMOUS— but most aren't dangerous to humans.

5

Octopus skin not only **CHANGES COLOR,** it also **CHANGES TEXTURE,** thanks to structures called papillae that can **GROW FROM SMALL TO TALL** in the blink of an eye.

6

Some octopuses carry around **COCONUT SHELL** halves to hide under when they feel threatened.

7

Octopuses are **NEAT FREAKS:** They clean the debris from their meals out of their dens daily.

8

Some octopuses tear off the **STINGING TENTACLES** of Portuguese man-of-wars and **WIELD THEM AS WEAPONS** (the octopuses themselves are immune to the sting).

IT'S THE BIGGEST BATTLE YET:

BLUE WHALES vs. *ARGENTINOSAURUS.*
This Earth-shaking smackdown across the ages imagines what could have been if these two beastly behemoths had ever crossed paths.

BLUE WHALE

> **THERE'S BIG**. And then there's the blue whale, the largest living animal by a long shot. These marine mammals can weigh as much as 28 adult African elephants, Earth's largest living land animal. And only a few sea-dwellers (a worm and a jellyfish, thanks to its tentacles) exceed a blue whale's length.

Blue whales swim through the world's oceans at speeds of 5 to 20 miles an hour (8–32 km/h), usually alone or in pairs. Not only are they large, they're also loud. These aquatic goliaths make low sounds to communicate with other blue whales as far as 1,000 miles (1,609 km) away!

BLUE WHALE VS ARGENTINOSAURUS

ARGENTINOSAURUS

> **TO FIND A WORTHY CONTENDER** for biggest beast, you have to travel back in time, almost 100 million years. That's when one of the biggest dinosaurs ever, *Argentinosaurus,* walked the earth.

Argentinosaurus fossils were first discovered in Argentina (as you may have guessed) in the 1980s. Scientists estimated it weighed an astounding 80 tons (73 t). Since then, its size has captured the attention of both experts and the public. Perhaps even more amazing: This big beast bulked up on plants alone!

DOES THE BIGGEST ANIMAL EVER SWIM IN OUR SEAS TODAY? Or did the largest megabeast to walk the Earth die out with the dinosaurs? Deciding which enormous animal is the winner is a BIG decision.

BLUE WHALES ARE AMONG THE **LONGEST LIVED** ANIMALS ALIVE TODAY. THEY CAN LIVE TO **AGE 90!**

BLUE WHALES bulk up by eating tiny animals called krill. These shrimp-like crustaceans are only a couple inches (5 cm) long. But blue whales scoop up and eat as much as **FOUR TONS** (3.6 t) **A DAY!** To do it, they use the baleen—a structure like a big comb attached to their upper jaw. The whales take a **BIG GULP OF WATER** and then squeeze it out through the baleen—leaving the krill behind to swallow.

BIG BABIES
Blue whales are big babies—literally. At birth, they already weigh about three tons (2.7 t) and are about 25 feet (7.6 m) long. For much of their first year, they rely on mother's milk and pack on weight at an astonishing rate: up to 200 pounds (90 kg) a day!

BIG BODY PARTS
You've read how big blue whales are. But you may be surprised that some of their body parts come in size XXL, too. Their tongues alone can be as big as a full-grown African elephant! When a whale washed ashore in Canada in 2014, scientists dissected it and discovered its heart weighed about 400 pounds (181 kg)!

BLUE WHALE

WINNER

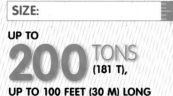

| COMMON NAME: | BLUE WHALE | SCIENTIFIC NAME: | BALAENOPTERA MUSCULUS |

SIZE:

UP TO
200 TONS (181 T),
UP TO 100 FEET (30 M) LONG

WHERE THEY LIVE:

OCEANS
WORLDWIDE

ARGENTINOSAURUS

| COMMON NAME: | ARGENTINOSAURUS | SCIENTIFIC NAME: | ARGENTINOSAURUS |

SIZE:

AROUND 80 TONS (73 T), MORE THAN

120 FEET (37 M) LONG

WHERE THEY LIVED:

PRESENT-DAY

ARGENTINA

STARTING SMALL

For their size, *Argentinosaurus* didn't start out so big. These dinos laid eggs only about the size of a coconut! Scientists know this thanks to an ancient giant nesting site with fossilized remains of some tens of thousands of eggs laid over many millennia.

AMAZINGLY, *Argentinosaurus* bulked up on plants. **A LOT OF PLANTS.** And all those plants made for **A LOT OF POOP.** Lucky for us, scientists have estimated how much: These dinos dropped about four gallons (15 L) of poop at a time! **LOOK OUT BELOW!**

LORDS OF THE LAND

Not only was *Argentinosaurus* one of the biggest dinos ever, it's also among the largest land animals ever. It weighed 11 times as much as an African elephant! Only a few fossils of *Argentinosaurus* have been found. But they're gargantuan: The dino's vertebrae (those bumps along your backbone) each stood five feet (1.5 m) tall!

A RANCHER FOUND THE FIRST *ARGENTINOSAURUS.* HE THOUGHT THE **OLD BONE** WAS A MASSIVE PIECE OF WOOD.

Tip to tail, *Argentinosaurus* was longer than blue whales are. But the whales weigh way more than the dinos: more than twice as much! That big difference is why blue whales are known as not only the largest living animals but also the largest animals ever! **WINNER: WHALES!**

EXTREME-LY BIG
BIG ANIMAL FACTS

BIG ... BIGGER ...
BIGGEST!

Pay attention, because these fun facts are a really BIG deal.

COCONUT CRAB

This **COLOSSAL CRAB** has big bragging rights: It's the **WORLD'S LARGEST LAND INVERTEBRATE.** It gets its name from its ability to punch holes in coconuts. The pinching force of this crab's meaty claws is **ALMOST EQUAL TO THE FORCE OF A LION'S BITE!**

LONG-EARED JERBOA

> When it comes to **BIGGEST EARS** for body size, this critter takes the cake. The rodent's ears are about half the length of its four-inch (10-cm)-long body! Think how odd you would look if your ears were half as tall as you!

CHINESE GIANT SALAMANDER

> **THIS SUPERSIZE AMPHIBIAN**—the world's largest—is **2,000 TIMES HEAVIER** and **10 TIMES LONGER** than the average salamander. So how big is it? It can reach six feet (1.8 m) long and weigh more than 25 pounds (11 kg)!

COMMON SHREW

> This mini mammal can pig out with the best of them: It eats as much as **90 PERCENT** of its body weight every day. **TALK ABOUT A BIG APPETITE!**

ANT

> If you've ever thought there seem to be an **AWFUL LOT OF ANTS,** you're right: There are more ants—**ABOUT 10 THOUSAND TRILLION**—than any other animal on Earth. (For comparison, there are only about 7 billion humans on Earth—that's 1.4 billion ants for every person.)

MOST PLAYFUL

ANIMAL LIFE ISN'T ONLY ABOUT FINDING FOOD AND FLEEING PREDATORS—

some like to play and have fun, too! When it comes to having a good time, **JAPANESE MACAQUES** and **RATS** are real-life party animals!

JAPANESE MACAQUE

➤ **HIGH IN THE MOUNTAINS** of Japan there's some serious monkey business. The freezing, snowy landscape is home to Japanese macaques, small, superfurry, pink-faced monkeys that have found a number of ways to have fun during the frigid winters.

These monkeys live in large groups of about 40 individuals, though sometimes the groups swell in size to more than 150 monkeys. They live as far up as 5,000 feet (1.5 km), higher than any primate other than humans, and can tolerate subzero temperatures!

RAT

> **RATS MAY NOT** first come to mind when thinking about animals that have fun. But wait until you finish reading about these rodents' sense of humor and love of games. There's much more to rats than scurrying and squeaking.

There are many species of rats, but the ones we'll focus on here are called Norway or brown rats. They live all over the planet, especially wherever people are, and are typically the species of rats scientists study and people keep as pets.

JAPANESE MACAQUE

★ **VS** ★

RAT

WHO WOULD YOU RATHER SPEND A SATURDAY WITH— a Japanese macaque or a rat? These two animals know how to have fun!

JAPANESE MACAQUES SOMETIMES WASH THEIR FOOD IN **SEAWATER** TO GIVE IT A **SALTY** FLAVOR.

LIKE ANY KID, young Japanese macaques **LOVE A GOOD GAME OF CHASE!** They also have **WRESTLING MATCHES** with each other. Though the animals are having fun, these games are also good practice for **THE REAL FIGHTS** they'll face in life.

HOT TUBBIN'

Hot tubs aren't just for humans: Japanese macaques take toasty dips, too! Instead of a man-made tub, though, these monkeys soak in steaming hot springs. The water in these naturally occurring, rocky hot tubs is heated to temperatures above 100°F (38°C) by volcanic forces beneath the earth. In the winter, macaques have a massive monkey pool party.

JAPANESE MACAQUE

COMMON NAME:	JAPANESE MACAQUE	SCIENTIFIC NAME:	MACACA FUSCATA

SIZE:

UP TO **25** POUNDS (11 KG), **LESS THAN** **2** FEET (0.6 M) TALL

WHERE THEY LIVE:

JAPAN

SNOW MUCH FUN!

People aren't the only animals that like to play with snowballs: Japanese macaques do, too! As babies, macaques figure out how to form balls, roll them downhill, and play keep-away. They like to roll and tumble in the soft snow, too. With their small stature and fluffy fur, they look like kids in snow coats!

CRAZY FOR GAMES

People keep rats as pets for a reason: They're pretty smart, and they're playful. One way you can play with a pet rat: by wrestling with it. A rat's no match for a person, but they love to tackle a wriggling hand, much like a kitten does. They'll also play tug-of-war, peek-a-boo, and hide-and-seek with people!

TRICKY RATS

Rats can be trained to do tricks—just like dogs! They can be taught to sit up, fetch, jump through a hoop, and more. One rat owner even taught his rodent buddy how to ride a custom-built surfboard!

IT MAY SOUND FUNNY, but rats are ticklish! We know this thanks to scientists who have TICKLED RATS while monitoring the animals' brain activity. Like people, rats don't like to be tickled when they're stressed, but FIND IT FUNNY when they're in a good mood. How can you tell when a rat finds something funny? They laugh! Rat giggles are too high-pitched for humans to hear, but a special machine can sense them.

RAT

| COMMON NAME: | NORWAY OR BROWN RAT | SCIENTIFIC NAME: | RATTUS NORVEGICUS |

SIZE:

UP TO
10 INCHES
(25 CM) LONG,
ABOUT 12 OUNCES (350 G)

WHERE THEY LIVE:

EVERYWHERE EXCEPT
ANTARCTICA

RATS **WILL EAT ANYTHING,** INCLUDING **GARBAGE** AND DEAD ANIMALS.

Rats do a lot of fun things. But Japanese macaques take it to the next level, having hot tub parties and playing with snowballs! So who would be the best to pal around with? **ALL THAT MONKEY BUSINESS MAKES MACAQUES THE WINNERS!**

FASTEST

QUICK:
WHAT'S THE FASTEST ANIMAL IN THE WORLD?

You're about to meet two contenders, **CHEETAHS** and **PEREGRINE FALCONS**, whose speeds on land and in the air make for one rapid race. Don't blink, or you might miss it!

CHEETAH

> **CHEETAHS** leave all other animals in the dust when it comes to running. These cats can cover up to 26 feet (8 m) in a single stride, which comes in handy during their high-speed, short chases. Cheetahs tire quickly, so they typically stalk their prey from behind tall grass and termite mounds before springing into action.

These fleet felines live across most of Africa and in Iran, but their numbers are declining, concerning scientists and cat-lovers alike. The most important race for cheetahs is the one to survive the next century.

PEREGRINE FALCON

> **PEREGRINE FALCONS** are the fighter jets of the animal kingdom. They're the fastest fliers on Earth, able to nab other birds and bats midair before their prey ever see them coming. They live on every continent except Antarctica and in all types of habitats, from deserts to big city bridges.

   People have trained peregrine falcons for hunting for thousands of years. Pesticides put the birds in peril last century, but they've since made a strong comeback.

CHEETAH
VS
PEREGRINE FALCON

IN THE ANIMAL OLYMPICS, would a cheetah or a peregrine falcon go home with the gold for fastest?

CHEETAHS HAVE TO HIDE THEIR CATCHES AND EAT **QUICKLY**— LIONS STEAL THEIR FOOD!

FAST FACTS

Cheetahs are the fastest animals on land. They can accelerate from 0 to 60 miles an hour (96.5 km/h) in just three seconds, and then maintain that superspeed over short distances. They can run 100 meters (328 feet) in 5.95 seconds—about 3.5 seconds faster than an Olympic gold-medal sprinter.

Cheetahs have **ANOTHER TRICK** when it comes to making **FAST TRACKS:** enlarged nostrils, lungs, and hearts. These BIG BODY PARTS let them draw in a lot of oxygen, which means more FUEL for their muscles to achieve their HIGH SPEEDS!

BUILT FOR SPEED

Like a fast car, cheetahs have a streamlined shape that helps them move through the air with as little resistance as possible. Superstrong hind leg and back muscles power sudden bursts of speed, and their flexible spines and long limbs allow for big strides. The fast cats keep from taking a tumble thanks to claws that help them grip the ground, and their long tails act as rudders to help them make sharp turns.

CHEETAH

COMMON NAME:	CHEETAH	SCIENTIFIC NAME:	ACINONYX JUBATUS

SIZE:

WHERE THEY LIVE:

UP TO ABOUT 7 FEET (2.1 M) LONG,

UP TO **143** POUNDS (65 KG)

AFRICA, IRAN

PEREGRINE FALCON

WINNER

COMMON NAME:	PEREGRINE FALCON	SCIENTIFIC NAME:	FALCO PEREGRINUS

SIZE:

UP TO ABOUT
19 INCHES
(48 CM) LONG;

WINGSPAN UP TO ABOUT 3.5 FEET (1 M)

WHERE THEY LIVE:

EVERYWHERE
EXCEPT ANTARCTICA

This bird's body is made to **SLICE THROUGH THE SKIES.** For starters, it has a big breastbone that supports big chest muscles. More muscle there means **MORE POWERFUL WING BEATS.** The shape of the falcon's wings plays a part, too: They're long and pointed, making them aerodynamic.

DAREDEVIL DIVES

Peregrine falcons are the fastest animals in the air. One way they kill prey is by swooping down on them in superfast dives called stoops. During these dives, the falcons fold their wings against their bodies and tuck in their feet. They drop as far as 3,000 feet (0.9 km) and reach speeds of more than 200 miles an hour (320 km/h)!

FLIGHT SUIT

It's hard to catch your breath while rocketing through the air at 200 miles an hour. But peregrine falcons have a special body part that helps them breathe while speeding: Cone-shaped structures in their nostrils help control the air flowing into their nose during superfast flight. Transparent third eyelids act like a pair of natural goggles.

A SCIENTIST STUDIED PEREGRINE FALCON **FLIGHT BY SKYDIVING** ALONGSIDE THE BIRDS.

Cheetahs are the fastest animals on land, but when it comes to top speed, peregrine falcons are faster. These birds reach speeds in the air more than double what the cats can do on land. So in the end, this race isn't even close. **WINNER: PEREGRINE FALCONS!**

EXTREME-LY FAST ANIMALS

MORE QUICK CRITTERS

These animals have a NEED FOR SPEED!

OSTRICH
This big bird can run **40 MILES AN HOUR** (64 km/h) and cover 16 feet (4.8 m) in a single stride.

STAR-NOSED MOLE
⬆ This **ODD-LOOKING MAMMAL** eats its food in less than a quarter of a second.

PLAINS SPADEFOOT TOAD

These **AMPHIBIANS** hatch from their eggs just two days after they're laid.

FRUIT FLY

These **TEENY-TINY INSECTS** can flap their wings more than **200 TIMES A SECOND!**

CAMEL

SURPRISE: A CAMEL CAN OUTRUN A HORSE! The desert dwellers can run about 25 miles an hour (40 km/h) for more than 20 miles (32 km), while horses can only keep up a pace of about 10.5 miles an hour (17 km/h) over long distances.

SONGBIRD AND STARLING

The muscles in the throats of songbirds and European starlings **MOVE A HUNDRED TIMES FASTER** than you can **BLINK YOUR EYE!** These superspeedy muscles make them **SUPERB SINGERS!**

ANIMALS USE TRICKERY, TEETH, VENOM,

and more to defend themselves and their territories at all costs. But these two fearsome fighters take it to the next level. In a fight between a GRIZZLY BEAR and BLACK MAMBA, which critter would make it out alive to claim the title of Deadliest Animal?

GRIZZLY BEAR

> **GRIZZLY BEARS ARE A TYPE OF BROWN BEAR,** and the biggest in the continental United States and Canada. They eat mostly fruits, nuts, and roots—but don't get on their bad side. When hungry or threatened, they're also known to chow down on animals—even supersize ones such as moose.

Grizzlies are largely loners, except for females and their cubs. They spend their lives roaming, some traveling 2,000 miles (3,219 km) in search of food. Moms are fiercely protective of their young—the reason for the phrase "mama bear"! And these bears are tough: Grizzlies survive below-freezing temperatures in the winter by hibernating (a sort of months-long sleep) in dens.

BLACK MAMBA 2

> **HOW INTIMIDATING** is a black mamba? Well, there's its coffin-shaped head (creepy!). Then there's its mouth, which the snake opens wide when threatened to reveal an eerie, pitch-black interior (hence its name). Then consider that this snake is speedy, extremely venomous, and on top of that, it's tenacious: Once attacked, this snake doesn't stop!

Black mambas live in Africa, where they're one of the most feared snakes. They're carnivores, consuming mostly mammals and birds, and occasionally cobras and other snakes. If they feel threatened, they will attack animals many times their own size, including humans.

GRIZZLY BEAR
★ VS ★
BLACK MAMBA

DEATH BY SNAKEBITE OR BEAR BITE? You choose after reading more about these killer creatures.

A GRIZZLY BEAR DOESN'T **PEE OR POOP** THE WHOLE TIME WHILE **HIBERNATING.**

BRUTAL BITE

Grizzly bears have big mouths: Wide-open it's almost a foot (30 cm) across! Their 42 teeth are formidable, too. They can crunch through bone in a single chomp—their bite force is strong enough to crush a bowling ball! And each of their four canines is about two inches (5 cm) long.

Have you ever seen a **GRIZZLY BEAR'S CLAWS?** They're the stuff of **NIGHTMARES,** curved and sharp, with front claws about two to four inches (5-10 cm) in length. They're **PERFECT FOR DEFENSE** and digging for food. The way to tell if bear tracks belong to a grizzly (vs. a smaller, less aggressive black bear) is to see if the claw marks are at least a couple inches above each toe.

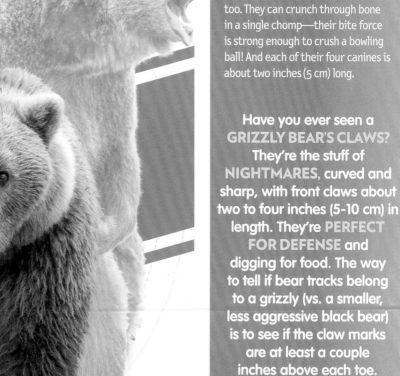

GRIZZLY BEAR

| COMMON NAME: | GRIZZLY BEAR, OR GRIZZLY | SCIENTIFIC NAME: | URSUS ARCTOS HORRIBILIS |

SIZE:

UP TO ABOUT
800 POUNDS (363 KG)

WHERE THEY LIVE:

CANADA AND THE **U.S.**

STATES OF ALASKA, MONTANA, IDAHO, AND WYOMING

CRUSHED TO DEATH

Grizzlies are very big animals, weighing up to 800 pounds. If all else fails, they can use their weight against their enemies, ramming them up against a tree or rock, or slamming into them and knocking them down (and out).

BLACK MAMBA

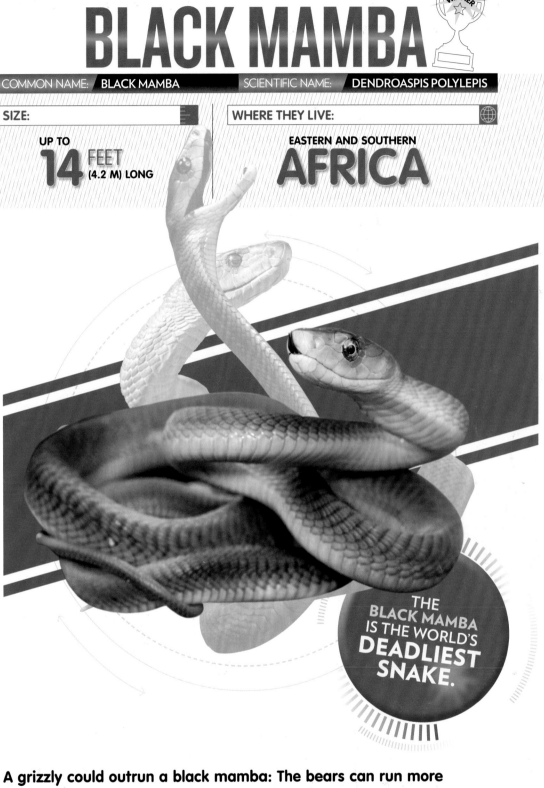

| COMMON NAME: | BLACK MAMBA | SCIENTIFIC NAME: | DENDROASPIS POLYLEPIS |

SIZE:

UP TO
14 FEET
(4.2 M) LONG

WHERE THEY LIVE:

EASTERN AND SOUTHERN
AFRICA

THE BLACK MAMBA IS THE WORLD'S **DEADLIEST SNAKE.**

SPEEDY SNAKE

Black mambas have both speed and length going for them. They're one of the fastest snakes on Earth, slithering at up to 12.5 miles an hour (20 km/h)—about half as fast as an Olympic sprinter. And at 14 feet (4.2 m), they're the longest venomous snake in Africa.

BLACK MAMBAS are shy and will try to flee a threatening situation when possible. But once backed into a corner, **THEY WON'T BACK DOWN!** They'll raise about a third of their body up off the ground and **QUICKLY AND REPEATEDLY STRIKE,** delivering large loads of venom to ensure their safety.

VERY LETHAL VENOM

There's no snake venom more fast-acting than a black mamba's. Delivered by half-inch (13-mm)-long fangs, it can kill an adult human in as quickly as 20 minutes. Unless anti-venin is rapidly given, a venomous bite kills 100 percent of the time.

A grizzly could outrun a black mamba: The bears can run more than twice as fast as the snakes can slither. But in a battle, a black mamba's strike would be quick, accurate, and lethal. A bitten bear wouldn't stand a chance, while a snake might survive a grizzly attack.

WINNER: BLACK MAMBA!

EXTREME-LY DEADLY ANIMALS

DON'T TOUCH!

Keep your distance from these DEADLY ANIMALS!

POISON DART FROG

▶ This frog's **BRIGHTLY COLORED SKIN** screams **"STAY AWAY!"** and for good reason: It secretes enough toxin to **KILL 10 HUMANS!**

BLUE-RINGED OCTOPUS

Less than eight inches (20 cm) in size, this octopus still packs a punch: **ITS VENOM CAN KILL A PERSON IN MINUTES!**

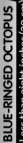

SOUTHERN CASSOWARY
At 130 pounds (59 kg) and with large, **RAZOR-SHARP CLAWS**, this big rain forest bird can **KILL WITH A SINGLE KICK!**

COMMON KINGSLAYER JELLYFISH
Though only a little more than an inch (2.5 cm) across, this **TINY JELLYFISH** delivers **STINGS THAT CAN KILL A PERSON.**

ANACONDA
This **SUPERSIZE SNAKE**—it weighs some 550 pounds (250 kg)—puts the **SQUEEZE ON ITS PREY**, suffocating them to death before **SWALLOWING THEM WHOLE!**

GEOGRAPHIC CONE SNAIL
Its patterned shell sure is pretty, but **DON'T PICK IT UP!** This snail's **VENOM PARALYZES PREY INSTANTLY** and is strong enough to kill humans.

HIPPOPOTAMUS
NEVER SURPRISE A HIPPO. When startled, it may turn its massive maw on you—these African animals kill more people than lions do!

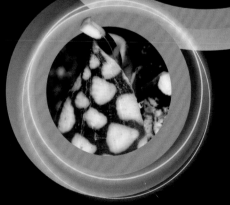

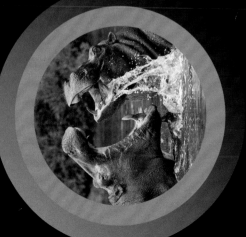

WEIRDEST

MOTHER NATURE HAS MADE A LOT OF *ANIMAL* ODDBALLS.

But two creatures in particular stand out from the peculiar pack. SPONGES are almost unrecognizable as animals. NAKED MOLE RATS break the rules about what it means to be a mammal. Prepare yourself: It's about to get weird.

SPONGE

>**SPONGES ARE SO UNLIKE** other animals that for a long time scientists thought they were plants. It's no wonder: Sponges don't really move, have no organs, no head, and no nervous system (so no brain).

But they do have skeletons (of a sort), bodies (simple ones), and they do eat—traits that make sponges just squeak into the animal category. Scientists estimate there are more than 10,000 species of sponges around the world, stuck to solid surfaces in both shallow and deep seawater and some freshwater, too.

NAKED MOLE RAT

> **ITS NAME IS NAKED MOLE RAT.** But these mammals are more closely related to guinea pigs and porcupines than they are to moles or rats. Their hairless bodies and oversize teeth put them in the "so ugly, it's cute" category.

 But the weirdness doesn't stop there. Naked mole rats live in insect-like colonies, are cold-blooded, and can survive long periods of time without oxygen, among other oddities.

SPONGE
VS
★   ★
NAKED MOLE RAT

NO BRAIN, NO ANIMAL? Sponges turn this idea on its head.
NO HAIR, NO MAMMAL? Naked mole rats confuse this concept.
This matchup has Earth's oddest animals face off in a clash of
the curious.

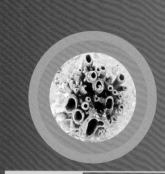

THE SKELETONS OF **SPONGES** ARE SOMETIMES USED AS CLEANING **SCRUBBERS.**

NO-BRAINER

Sponges have no brain—not even a single neuron, or nerve cell, in their entire body. Think about that (a sponge can't!). For comparison, a human brain has approximately 100 billion neurons, and a measly mouse brain about 75 million. Sponges are the only multicellular animal without a nervous system.

SPONGES typically **ATTACH THEMSELVES** to a solid surface and pretty much **STAY PUT FOR THE REST OF THEIR LIVES.** Despite having **NO BRAIN,** they've figured out a **CLEVER WAY TO EAT:** have their food come to them. The sponges wave tiny, whiplike structures to move the surrounding water through tiny pores in their bodies, **CAPTURING** every living thing floating in it.

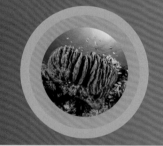

ODD BODIES

Sponges come in a wide variety of shapes, from tubes to spheres to tree-like structures. With no head or organs, those bodies are strange ones. But they do have a few familiar features—like skeletons. Instead of bone, though, they're made of silica, the main ingredient in glass.

SPONGE

WINNER

| COMMON NAME: | SPONGE | SCIENTIFIC NAME: | PORIFERA PHYLUM |

SIZE:

WHERE THEY LIVE:

0.5 INCH (1.3 CM) TO ALMOST **6** FEET (1.8 M)

SEAS AND FRESHWATER AROUND THE **WORLD**

NAKED MOLE RAT

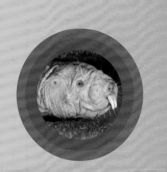

| COMMON NAME: | NAKED MOLE RAT | SCIENTIFIC NAME: | HETEROCEPHALUS GLABER |

SIZE:

ABOUT
6 INCHES
(15 CM) LONG,

TAIL INCLUDED

WHERE THEY LIVE:

UNDERGROUND, IN THE DESERTS OF
EAST AFRICA

NO HAIR, DON'T CARE

Having almost no hair isn't the norm for land mammals. But since the naked mole rat spends its whole life underground, it doesn't need hair to protect it from the sun. And it doesn't need a furry coat to help keep it warm, either. The animals live in belowground homes that stay around 85°F (29°C). That makes them cold-blooded, like reptiles.

LIVING LIKE INSECTS

Another way in which naked mole rats aren't your average mammal: They live in large colonies with a queen and workers and soldiers—like ants do! Up to 300 animals can live in a single colony. Soldiers spend their time protecting the colony, while workers dig chambers, find food (tubers they gnaw on with their long teeth), and care for the queen's young.

NAKED MOLE RATS made news in 2017 when SHOCKED SCIENTISTS discovered the rodents could survive 18 MINUTES WITHOUT OXYGEN just fine. (To give you an idea of how incredible that is, a mouse dies in less than a minute without oxygen.)

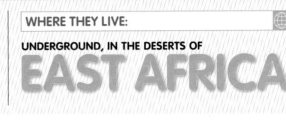

NAKED MOLE RATS **EAT THEIR OWN POOP,** TO GET MORE NUTRIENTS FROM THEIR FOOD.

Naked mole rats are undeniably weird. But sponges have no head, no brain—and no organs at all. They barely move. And yet, they're still animals. It just doesn't get any weirder than that. SO THE WINNER IS SPONGES!

EXTREME-LY *WEIRD ANIMALS*

MORE ANIMAL ODDBALLS

You're about to meet some of the most **WONDERFULLY WEIRD** animals ever!

CHINESE WATER DEER

⌃ This cute but **KINDA CREEPY DEER** vants to **SUCK YOUR BLOOD!** Not really: These herbivores use their long, curved canines for fighting.

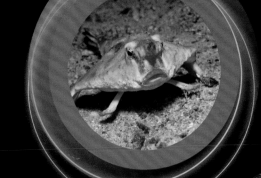

RED-LIPPED BATFISH

⌃ **PUCKER UP:** This sea creature's **BRIGHT RED LIPS** make it look like it's wearing lipstick!

GLASS LIZARD

TRUST US: This legless critter is really a lizard! It gets its name from its **EASILY BREAKABLE, SUPERLONG TAIL,** which grows back.

TURTLE FROG

∨ Upon first glance, this **KOOKY CREATURE** looks like a turtle that's lost its shell. Turns out it's actually a burrowing frog that spends almost its whole life **UNDERGROUND.**

HEMICERATOIDES HIEROGLYPHICA

∨ Some animals are **REALLY PICKY EATERS.** But they've got nothing on this moth from Madagascar: **IT EATS ONLY THE TEARS OF SLEEPING BIRDS,** which it slurps up with a specialized proboscis!

BIRD-DROPPING SPIDER

∧ This spider disguises itself by **LOOKING LIKE A PIECE OF BIRD POOP.** The tactic keeps the spider safe from predators and helps it hide from its favorite meal, moths, **UNTIL THE PREY IS NEAR ENOUGH TO NAB.**

LAZIEST

SLOOOOOOW BUT NOT SLEEPY: SLOTH   SLEEPING AND EATING THE DAY AWAY: KOALA

AT SOME POINT IN YOUR LIFE, YOU'VE PROBABLY BEEN CALLED LAZY.

But you're about to meet two animals, KOALAS and SLOTHS, that are so slow, it can be hard to tell if they're awake or asleep … or sometimes whether they're even alive!

SLOTH

> **SLOTHS** are so low-energy that their name is actually another word for laziness. And for a long time, scientists thought sloths slept most of the day. But recent studies on sloths in Panama found otherwise: Much of the time these animals appear to be asleep, they're actually awake. In fact, they sleep only about 9.6 hours a day. So sloths move slowly, but it seems they're not particularly sleepy.

There are two types of sloths, two-toed and three-toed. Both live in the forest canopies of Central and South America. For this battle, we'll focus on three-toed sloths.

KOALA

> **MANY PEOPLE CONSIDER THE KOALA** to be one of the cutest, cuddliest-looking critters around. But did you know koalas are also incredibly lazy animals? They spend most of their lives in eucalyptus trees, either eating or sleeping.

Koalas live only in eastern Australia. Their bodies are suited to very specific conditions that make for an extremely limited lifestyle.

CONGRATULATIONS! You mustered enough energy to turn the page! That's more than a koala or sloth would do.

SLOTHS MOVE MORE **SWIFTLY IN WATER** THAN ON LAND.

THREE-TOED SLOTH

COMMON NAME:	THREE-TOED SLOTH	SCIENTIFIC NAME:	BRADYPODIDAE FAMILY

SIZE:

1.5 TO 2 FEET (0.5-0.6 M) BODIES, TAILS THAT ARE ABOUT 2 INCHES (5 CM) LONG

WHERE THEY LIVE:

FOREST CANOPIES OF CENTRAL AND SOUTH **AMERICA**

LIFE IN SLOW-MO
Sloths take it easy. They spend much of their lives literally just hanging around, suspended from trees with their long, curved claws. When they do make a move, they travel only about 0.1 mile an hour (.16 km/h), or about nine feet (2.7 m) a minute! They're the slowest mammals in the world.

SLOTHS are so **SLOW** going, they can't even be bothered to poop more than once a week. It turns out that's a good thing: On the **FOREST FLOOR**, sloths are more **VULNERABLE TO PREDATORS**. And getting down and back takes a lot of energy **(FOR A SLOTH)**.

SLOW GROWING
Sloths move so little that algae (and fungi) grow on their fur. While it may sound gross, the algae are actually an advantage—they help the sloths blend in with their leafy green surroundings. And scientists have found algae in sloths' stomachs, so they may be a nutritional boost, too.

As you know by now, **KOALAS** like to keep things **SIMPLE**. Yet another way they do this: by getting most of the moisture they need from the **LEAVES THEY EAT.** In fact, koalas **RARELY DRINK WATER** at all! This handy trick lets them spend less time worrying about water and **MORE TIME SLEEPING.**

SERIOUS SLEEPYHEADS

Koalas are one of the sleepiest animals ever, dozing about 18 hours a day (almost twice as much as sloths). That means they're awake only about six hours a day, or only 25 percent of the time! And even when they are awake, don't expect a lot of action—koalas spend only about four minutes a day actually moving around.

PICKY EATERS

Imagine eating only one thing all day, every day. Then imagine sitting in that food while eating it, all day, every day. That's exactly what koalas do, taking up residence in trees, typically eucalyptus, where the leaves—their favorite meal— are in easy reach. Koalas rarely eat anything else or roam outside a forest filled with trees. They really love eucalyptus leaves!

KOALA

| COMMON NAME: | KOALA | SCIENTIFIC NAME: | PHASCOLARCTOS CINEREUS |

SIZE:

2-3 FEET (0.85 M) LONG,
ABOUT 20 POUNDS (9 KG)

WHERE THEY LIVE:

EASTERN
AUSTRALIA

THOUGH SOME CALL THEM KOALA BEARS, THEY'RE NOT **BEARS**— KOALAS ARE MARSUPIALS.

Believe it or not, there's something more sedentary than a sloth, and that's a koala. While sloths move slowly, at least they don't sleep most of their days away. **DESPITE THEIR NEAR-TOTAL LACK OF TRYING, KOALAS WIN THE TITLE OF LAZIEST ANIMAL.**

MILLIONS OF YEARS AGO,

CROCODILES twice the size of today's swam in an ancient sea that covered what is now the Sahara desert. Flying reptiles called **PTEROSAURS** with wingspans wider than an F-16 fighter jet's soared over the area now called Texas. Though these two beasts wouldn't have crossed paths in real life, in a prehistoric battle between the two, which would be the winner and which would go extinct?

QUETZALCOATLUS

> CAN YOU IMAGINE looking up and seeing a 16-foot (5-m) flying reptile soaring toward you? This was an everyday sight for dinosaurs that walked Earth about 70 million years ago. For some dinos, this fearsome flier—a pterosaur called *Quetzalcoatlus northropi*—was the last thing they ever saw...because it plucked them from the ground and gobbled them up.

Pterosaurs weren't birds or dinosaurs. They were ancient reptiles that were the first vertebrate (backboned) animals to fly, before birds and bats. They have no living descendants: Their kind went completely extinct millions of years ago. But they left behind bones that scientists have unearthed, studied, and assembled. These winged terrors have taught us that flying animals can be even bigger than we ever thought possible!

QUETZALCOATLUS VS SUPERCROC

★ VS ★

SUPERCROC

> **IF TODAY'S CROCODILES GIVE YOU THE CREEPS,** just wait until you read what their counterparts were like more than 100 million years ago. "SuperCroc," an ancient megacroc, was as big as a bus!

SuperCroc made world headlines in 2001, when scientists announced they had found fossils in the Sahara that revealed just how humongous this creature was. The 40-foot (12-m) long reptile lived in rivers and feasted on fish and any other animals—including small dinosaurs—it could get its jumbo jaws on.

THIS ANCIENT BATTLE IS BETWEEN TWO ANIMALS, one aquatic and one aerial. Where will they fight it out? In the sky, or in the water?

QUETZALCOATLUS COULD FOLD UP ITS WINGS AND **"WALK"** ON ALL FOURS.

QUETZALCOATLUS

COMMON NAME: **QUETZALCOATLUS**   SCIENTIFIC NAME: **QUETZALCOATLUS NORTHROPI**

SIZE:

WHERE THEY LIVED:

16 FEET (5 M) TALL,

WINGSPAN OF 36 FEET (11 M)

PRESENT-DAY

NORTH AMERICA

BIG BEAK

Quetzalcoatlus had no teeth, but it didn't really need them. Its beak was six feet (1.8 m) long, or about the size of an adult human male. Scientists say the beast likely plucked small dinosaurs and other fox-size animals off the ground to eat after spying them from above.

At **16 FEET** (5 m) **TALL** and weighing some **550 POUNDS** (250 kg), *QUETZALCOATLUS* looked like a **NIGHTMARE** version of a **GIANT STORK.** It was about as tall as a giraffe and as heavy as a male lion. It's one of the **BIGGEST ANIMALS EVER** to have taken to the sky.

SUPERSIZE WINGS

Today, the wandering albatross has the largest wingspan of any living bird: 11 feet (3.3 m) across! But *Quetzalcoatlus* puts it to shame: The beast's wingspan was a real whopper at 36 feet (11 m) across! A superlong fourth finger supported each of *Quetzalcoatlus*'s wings. It could fly some 10,000 miles (16,000 km) non-stop, about the distance from London to Beijing and back!

JAW-SOME!

SuperCroc's jaws alone were six feet (1.8 m) long. As if that weren't scary enough, those jaws were lined with more than 100 teeth that one scientist likened to "railroad spikes," including incisors that could crush bones.

SUIT OF ARMOR

SuperCroc had a supertough exterior. Bony structures called scutes, each about a foot (0.3 m) long, covered and shielded its neck, back, and tail. Although SuperCroc is no longer around, scutes can still be found on today's crocs, turtles, and other animals.

SUPERCROC WAS SUPER, all right. At **40 FEET** (12 m) long and **17,500 POUNDS** (8 t), it was twice as long as today's **BIGGEST CROCS** and more than six times their weight! Most of its bulk stayed hidden beneath the water, scientists think, as the croc's eyes **PEEKED ABOVE** and scanned the water for something to **SNACK ON.**

SUPERCROC

| COMMON NAME: | SUPERCROC | SCIENTIFIC NAME: | SARCOSUCHUS IMPERATOR |

SIZE:

40 FEET (12 M) LONG

WHERE THEY LIVED:

PRESENT-DAY
SAHARA

SUPERCROC **WEIGHED** AS MUCH AS **TWO** ELEPHANTS.

Both prehistoric animals are pretty awesome. And their big jaws are the same size. But SuperCroc is the one with teeth—lots of 'em—and it has about 17,000 pounds (7.8 t) on *Quetzalcoatlus*. IT SEEMS FAIR TO SAY THAT SUPERCROC WOULD HAVE LITERALLY CRUSHED THE COMPETITION!

LEVIATHANS FROM LONG AGO

PREHISTORIC VS. PRESENT-DAY ANIMALS

Time travel to the past to learn about these ancient—AND EXTRA-LARGE—VERSIONS OF PRESENT-DAY ANIMALS!

TITANOBOA CERREJONENSIS

If you think today's snakes are big, check out what slithered across Earth 60 million years ago: *Titanoboa cerrejonensis* was 42 feet (13 m) long, weighed 2,500 pounds (1,135 kg), and is **THE LARGEST SNAKE EVER!**

GRIFFINFLY

Dragonfly-like griffinflies, which lived about 300 million years ago, could be real whoppers: The biggest of these bugs had **WINGSPANS OF 27 INCHES** (0.7 m)—**THAT'S JUST OVER TWO FEET!**

JAEKELOPTERUS RHENANIAE

⌃ This **SUPERSIZE RELATIVE** of today's **SEA SCORPIONS** was 8.2 feet (2.5 m) long—**FAR BIGGER THAN A HUMAN!** It swam in freshwater, instead of seas, some 400 million years ago and **RIPPED ITS PREY TO SHREDS** with 1.5-foot (46-cm) claws!

JOSEPHOARTIGASIA MONESI

⌄ Today's rodents would have been no match for the ones that **STOMPED**, instead of scurried, a few million years ago: *Josephoartigasia monesi* was **AS BIG AS A BULL**, weighing 2,200 pounds (1,000 kg). Its skull alone was nearly two feet (0.6 m) long. **EEK!**

BEELZEBUFO AMPINGA

⌃ That's no beach ball—**IT'S A GIANT FROG!** This 70-million-year-old amphibian stood (or squatted, rather) 16 inches (41 cm) high and weighed about 10 pounds (4.5 kg). It was bigger than the largest living frog, **THE GOLIATH FROG**, whose weight tops out at 7 pounds (3 kg).

BEST COMPANION

IT'S PERHAPS THE *ULTIMATE* ANIMAL SMACKDOWN:

DOGS vs. **CATS**, for the bragging right of best pet. Forget which team you may think you're on. Keep reading to find out fascinating facts that give each contender a fighting chance.

CAT

> **ABOUT 8,000 YEARS AGO,** cats were hanging around farming communities and earning their keep by catching rodents. Some 4,000 years ago, ancient Egyptians were feeding and housing wild cats, treating them as pets. In fact, they took it one step further, viewing their feline companions as gods and building an entire city and temples to worship them!

Like dogs, cats come in many sizes, shapes, and colors, but they all belong to one species. All are built to stalk, prey, and pounce, though of course some choose not to and instead spend most of their time snoozing in a sunny spot indoors.

DOG

> **MORE THAN 30,000 YEARS AGO,** wolves began hanging around humans and developed such a close relationship with them that they stopped being wild and instead became pets. Today we call these domesticated animals dogs.

There are many types, or breeds, of dog, and they can look very different from each other (think of a Chihuahua and a Great Dane). They can also have very different temperaments, from feisty to sweet, and very different skill sets and interests, such as herding and hunting. But all dogs belong to a single species. And all dogs are inherently interested in humans, the animals upon whom they rely.

★ CAT VS DOG ★

WHICH WOULD YOU RATHER HAVE FOR A FRIEND: the pet that purrs or the one that wags its tail? Only one can win this age-old battle of humans' best bud!

BIG CATS LIKE LIONS AND TIGERS CAN'T **PURR.**

CAT

COMMON NAME:	CAT	SCIENTIFIC NAME:	FELIS CATUS

SIZE:

5-20 POUNDS (2-9 KG)

WHERE THEY LIVE:

EVERYWHERE ON EARTH

GOOD VIBRATIONS

A cat's purring may be the best thing about it. That soft sound coming from a contented cat snuggled up against you can be so soothing. Vibrating muscles in a cat's voice box cause the sound. Scientists now think cats purr not only when they're content but also when they're injured or sick, to self-soothe or attract attention.

CATS can hear a wider range of sounds than both people and pooches. They especially excel at hearing **HIGH-PITCHED SOUNDS,** including those beyond human and dog hearing. A human can hear sound up to 20,000 hertz (a measurement of how high or low pitched a sound is), a dog up to twice that, and cats up to three times that, topping out at about **60,000 HERTZ.**

CATS DO CARE

Cats are famous for their "cattitude." Sometimes it may seem like they don't care much about their human companions. But a recent study found otherwise. When given a choice, the majority of cats in the study picked interacting with people over food and toys.

TRAINED TRICKSTERS

Dogs can be trained to do extraordinary things, everything from riding a skateboard to helping people with disabilities get around. A recent study found that dogs' desire to please isn't limited to people. They like to help other dogs, too. In a test, dogs chose to give food to their furry friends, even when they didn't get a treat themselves. How sweet!

EXCELLENT EYESIGHT

Dogs can see things superfast, about 1.4 times faster than people do. They can process visual information—say a light flashing—about 25 percent faster than humans, a study found. This means dogs see things happen in slow motion, helping them react. Cats, for comparison, see 1.1 times slower than people.

You probably feel like you can tell when your **DOGGY FRIEND** is happy or bummed out. And science agrees. Studies have shown that people can tell whether a dog is being **PLAYFUL OR PROTECTIVE** just by hearing its **BARK.**

DOG
WINNER

| COMMON NAME: | DOG | SCIENTIFIC NAME: | CANIS LUPUS FAMILIARIS |

SIZE:

3-75 POUNDS
(1-34 KG)

WHERE THEY LIVE:

EVERYWHERE ON EARTH

DOGS HAVE ABOUT **220 MILLION** SCENT RECEPTORS, OR CELLS THAT SENSE SMELLS.

Both cats and dogs can be great companions. But dogs don't have "cattitude." And dogs and people go way back—in fact, the canines were bred to be humans' besties, snuggling, fetching, and showering us with love. **SO, SORRY CAT-LOVERS, THE WINNER OF THIS BIG BATTLE: DOGS!**

EXTREME-LY COOL CATS AND DOGS

THESE PETS PROVE SOME CATS AND DOGS ARE CAPABLE OF MUCH MORE THAN THE USUAL PARTY TRICKS!

MAYOR MEOW
Stubbs, **A PEACH-COLORED TAILLESS CAT,** served as **HONORARY MAYOR** of the small Alaska, U.S.A., town of Talkeetna **FOR 20 YEARS.**

RESCUE RACERS
Trainers in Auckland, New Zealand, taught three rescue dogs **HOW TO DRIVE** around a racetrack. (**DON'T WORRY:** The pooches' modified automobile has a top speed of only 7.5 miles an hour [12 km/h]!)

PAINTING POOCH

Sammy, a **FOXHOUND/SHEPHERD MIX** from Maryland, U.S.A., **PAINTS PICTURES** (by holding a brush in his mouth) that sell for as much as $1,700 each.

LENDING A PAW

Milo, a **TERRIER MIX IN WALES, U.K.,** acts as a **GUIDE DOG FOR HIS BFF, EDDY,** a black Lab who went blind while the two were buddies.

ULTIMATE ANIMAL BRACKET

ALL OF THE ANIMALS IN THIS BOOK ARE AWESOME, but only half are winners, and only one is the Ultimate Animal! By now you've read each animal's strengths and weaknesses, but could you correctly guess which would best all others if the winners went head-to-head?

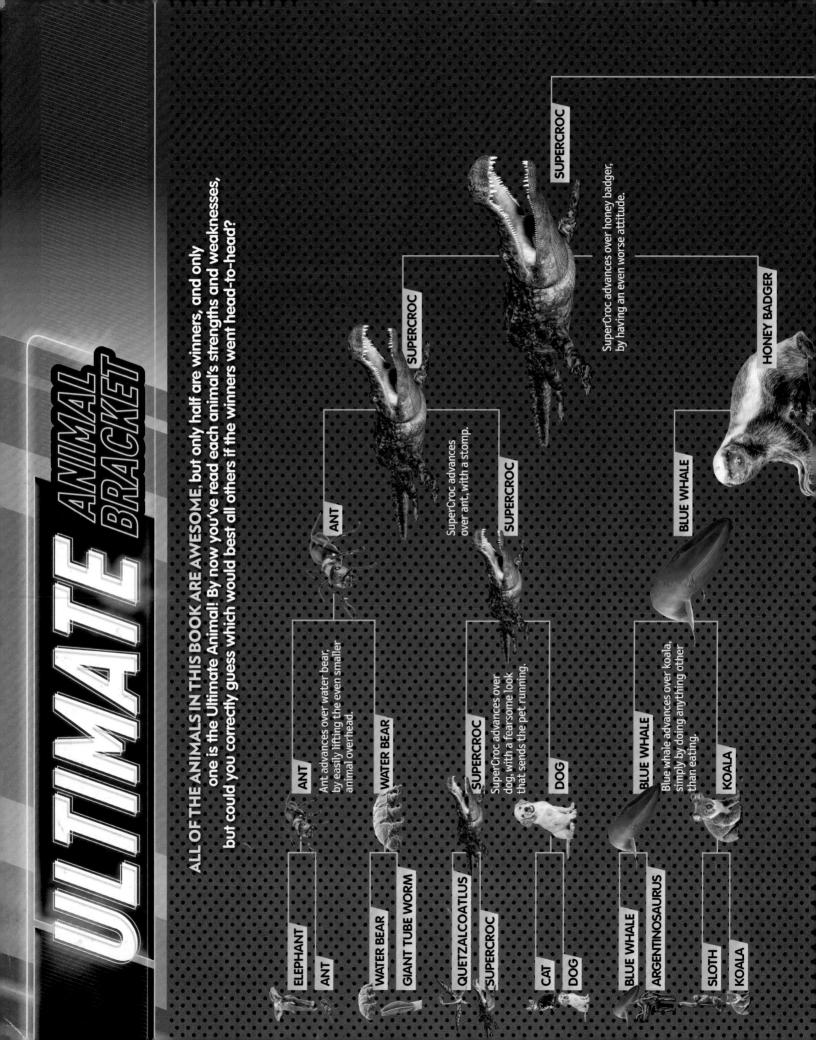

SUPERCROC

SuperCroc advances over honey badger, by having an even worse attitude.

HONEY BADGER

SUPERCROC

ANT

SuperCroc advances over ant, with a stomp.

SUPERCROC

BLUE WHALE

Ant advances over water bear, by easily lifting the even smaller animal overhead.

ANT

WATER BEAR

SUPERCROC

SuperCroc advances over dog, with a fearsome look that sends the pet running.

DOG

BLUE WHALE

Blue whale advances over koala, simply by doing anything other than eating.

KOALA

ELEPHANT
ANT

WATER BEAR
GIANT TUBE WORM

QUETZALCOATLUS
SUPERCROC

CAT
DOG

BLUE WHALE
ARGENTINOSAURUS

SLOTH
KOALA

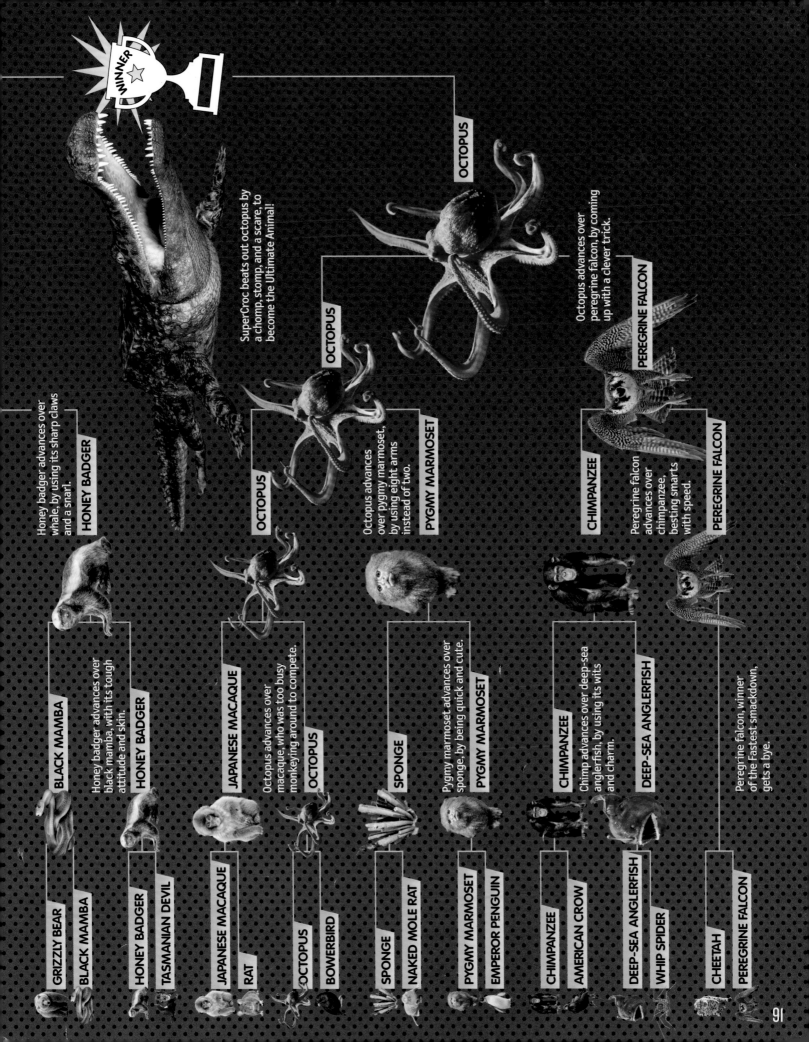

WINNER

SuperCroc beats out octopus by a chomp, stomp, and a scare, to become the Ultimate Animal!

OCTOPUS

OCTOPUS

Octopus advances over peregrine falcon, by coming up with a clever trick.

PEREGRINE FALCON

Honey badger advances over whale, by using its sharp claws and a snarl.

HONEY BADGER

OCTOPUS

Octopus advances over pygmy marmoset, by using eight arms instead of two.

PYGMY MARMOSET

CHIMPANZEE

Peregrine falcon advances over chimpanzee, besting smarts with speed.

PEREGRINE FALCON

BLACK MAMBA

Honey badger advances over black mamba, with its tough attitude and skin.

HONEY BADGER

JAPANESE MACAQUE

Octopus advances over macaque, who was too busy monkeying around to compete.

OCTOPUS

SPONGE

Pygmy marmoset advances over sponge, by being quick and cute.

PYGMY MARMOSET

CHIMPANZEE

Chimp advances over deep-sea anglerfish, by using its wits and charm.

DEEP-SEA ANGLERFISH

Peregrine falcon, winner of the Fastest smackdown, gets a bye.

GRIZZLY BEAR
BLACK MAMBA

HONEY BADGER
TASMANIAN DEVIL

JAPANESE MACAQUE
RAT

OCTOPUS
BOWERBIRD

SPONGE
NAKED MOLE RAT

PYGMY MARMOSET
EMPEROR PENGUIN

CHIMPANZEE
AMERICAN CROW

DEEP-SEA ANGLERFISH
WHIP SPIDER

CHEETAH
PEREGRINE FALCON

INDEX

CREDITS

CREDITS

Since 1888, the National Geographic Society has funded more than 12,000 research, exploration, and preservation projects around the world. The Society receives funds from National Geographic Partners, LLC, funded in part by your purchase. A portion of the proceeds from this book supports this vital work. To learn more, visit natgeo.com/info.

For more information, visit nationalgeographic.com, call 1-800-647-5463, or write to the following address:

National Geographic Partners
1145 17th Street N.W.
Washington, D.C. 20036-4688 U.S.A.

Visit us online at nationalgeographic.com/books

For librarians and teachers: ngchildrensbooks.org

More for kids from National Geographic: natgeokids.com

For information about special discounts for bulk purchases, please contact National Geographic Books Special Sales: specialsales@natgeo.com

For rights or permissions inquiries, please contact National Geographic Books Subsidiary Rights: bookrights@natgeo.com

Designed by Brett Challos

Hardcover ISBN: 978-1-4263-3151-0
Reinforced library binding ISBN: 978-1-4263- 3152-7

The publisher would like to acknowledge everyone who helped make this book possible: Ariane Szu-Tu, editor; Stephanie Warren Drimmer, project editor; Shannon Hibberd, senior photo editor; Christina Ascani, associate photo editor; Joan Gossett, production editor; and Gus Tello and Anne LeongSon, design production assistants.

Printed in China
18/RRDS/2

ALL OF THE ANIMALS IN THIS BOOK ARE UNIQUE AND AMAZING! BUT I'D OBVIOUSLY WIN IF THERE WAS A "BEAUTY" CATEGORY.